A Visit to
SCOTLAND

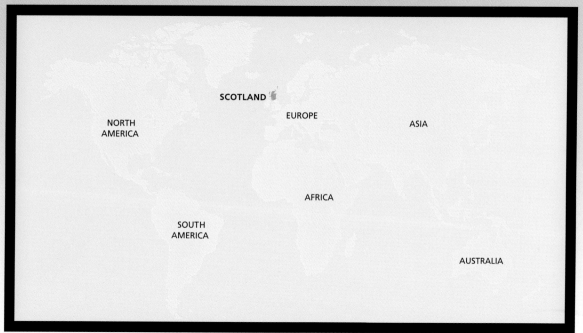

Chris Oxlade and Anita Ganeri

Heinemann Library
Chicago, Illinois

Designed by Ron Kamen and StoreyBooks
Originated by Dot Gradations Ltd.
Printed in China by South China Printing Company

07 06 05 04 03
10 9 8 7 6 5 4 3 2 1

Library of Congress Cataloging-in-Publication Data
Ganeri, Anita, 1961-
  Scotland / Anita Ganeri and Chris Oxlade.
      v. cm. -- (A visit to)
Includes bibliographical references and index.
Contents: Scotland -- Land -- Landmarks -- Homes -- Food -- Clothes -- Work -- Transportation -- Language -- School -- Free time -- Celebrations -- The arts -- Fact file.
  ISBN 1-40340-966-8 (library binding-hardcover)
  1. Scotland--Juvenile literature. [1. Scotland.] I. Oxlade, Chris.
II. Title. III. Series.
  DA762 .G28 2002
  941.1086--dc21

                              2002007409
Acknowledgments
The author and publishers are grateful to the following for permission to reproduce copyright material: pp. 5, 6, 7, 8, 9, 10, 11, 12, 18, 19, 20, 21, 23, 24, 25 Peter Evans; p. 13 Food Features; p. 14 Collections/Dorothy Burrows; p. 15 Collections/Julian Nieman; p. 16 Trip/C. Sanders; p. 17 Collections/George Wright; p. 22 Trip/S. Grant; p. 26 Trip/A. Tovy; p. 27 Scottish Viewpoint; p. 28 Trip/G. Hancock; p. 29 Collections/Graham Burns. Cover photograph of Eilean Donan Castle on Loch Duich, reproduced with permission of Corbis/Ray Juno.

Every effort has been made to contact copyright holders of any material reproduced in this book. Any omissions will be rectified in subsequent printings if notice is given to the publisher.

Some words are shown in bold, **like this.** You can find out what they mean by looking in the glossary.

Contents

Scotland

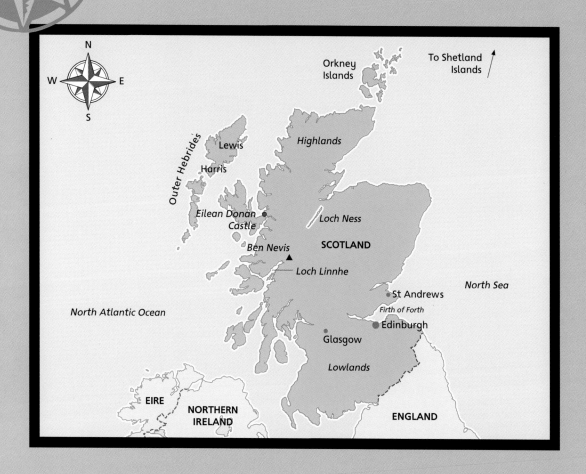

Scotland is a country in the United Kingdom. It is also part of a group of islands called the British Isles. About five million people live in Scotland.

The **capital** city of Scotland is called Edinburgh. Edinburgh has many old buildings. Edinburgh Castle stands on top of a hill, looking down over the city below.

Land

Scotland is a very beautiful country. In the south, there are gentle hills covered with forests and fields. This part of the country is called the **Lowlands.**

The northern and western areas of Scotland are called the **Highlands**. There are mountains, lakes called **lochs,** and valleys called glens. Off the west **coast,** there are many islands.

Landmarks

The Forth Railway Bridge carries trains over a body of water called the Firth of Forth. This famous bridge is over 100 years old.

Scotland has many pretty castles. This is
Eilean Donan Castle in the **Highlands**. It
stands on an island in the sea. People
still live in this castle.

Homes

Scottish people are called Scots. Most Scots live in Edinburgh, Glasgow, and other places in the **Lowlands.** Many people live in apartments in the cities.

People in the **Highlands** usually live in small villages. They can be a long way from the nearest town. Farmers used to live in **traditional** houses called *crofts*.

Food

There are lots of fish in Scotland's rivers. Some of them are salmon and trout, which are delicious to eat. Fish-farmers raise fish in farms on the **coast**.

Haggis is probably Scotland's most famous food. It is made of sheep's **innards** and oatmeal. Scots eat it with **neeps** and **tatties** or with french fries.

Clothes

Children in Scotland wear T-shirts, jeans, and sportswear at home or when they play with friends. Many children wear **uniforms** at school.

These men are wearing **traditional**
Scottish **kilts.** They are made from
tartan, a woolen cloth made in Scotland.
Many Scottish families have their own
tartan pattern.

Work

There is a lot of oil under the sea off Scotland's east **coast**. People live and work on **oil rigs** in the North Sea, pumping out the oil.

Many people in the **Highlands** and on the Scottish islands raise animals or make things at home. This woman is **spinning** wool for sweaters.

Transportation

Edinburgh and Glasgow are Scotland's busiest cities. Buses and trains bring many people to the cities to work every morning. Glasgow has an underground railway, too.

On the west **coast** of Scotland, **ferries** carry people, cars, buses, and trucks to the islands and across **lochs.** People then drive to where they want to go.

Language

Most Scots speak English, but many have their own **accent**. People from Glasgow may sound different from people who live in the **Highlands** when they speak English.

Fàilte gu
Iochdar Throdarnais
Welcome to Trotternish

All Tourist Services. Crafts.
Accommodation. Hotels.
Ferry to Western Isles.

In the Highlands, and on the islands of
Harris and Lewis, many people speak a
language called *Gaelic*. Signs are written in
both English and Gaelic.

School

Scottish children start school when they are four or five years old. They must go to school until they are sixteen years old. These children are at school in Edinburgh.

In tiny villages on the Scottish islands, there may only be a few children. They go to small schools with only one or two teachers.

Free Time

Golf was first played in Scotland. It is a very popular sport there. Children often start playing golf when they are very young.

Tourists come from all over the world to walk or climb in the Scottish **Highlands**. In the winter, the mountains are covered with snow. People ski on them.

Celebrations

Every summer, many Scottish people go to the **Highland** games. They might dance, sing, play **traditional** sports, or display things they have made.

Scots celebrate the birth of the Scottish poet Robert Burns with lots of fireworks on Burns Night, January 25. Many also hold parties on New Year's Eve, which the Scots call *Hogmanay*.

The Arts

Musicians called *pipers* play a **traditional** Scottish instrument, the bagpipes. It is a hard instrument to play well. Pipe bands often play at special occasions such as weddings.

The Edinburgh International Festival
takes place every August. Artists perform
plays, music, dance, and poetry all over
the city. It is the largest arts **festival** in
the world.

Fact File

Name	Scotland is part of the United Kingdom of Great Britain and Northern Ireland.
Capital	The **capital** city is Edinburgh.
Languages	English and Gaelic are the two official languages of Scotland.
Population	About five million people live in Scotland.
Money	Money is called pounds sterling. Its symbol is £.
Religion	The official Christian church of Scotland is called the Church of Scotland. There are other churches and some people follow other religions.
Products	Scotland produces oil and gas, electronics, chemicals, textiles, timber, barley, food, whiskey, and cattle. Tourism is important, too.

Scottish Gaelic Words You Can Learn

aon (say: ern)	one
dhà (say: dyarh)	two
trì (say: te-ree)	three
tha (say: haa)	yes
chan eil (say: han-yel)	no
hallo (say: hallo)	hello
mor sin leat (say: mar-shin-let)	goodbye
tapadh leat (say: tah-pu-let)	thank you

Glossary

accent	way words sound when people say them
capital	most important city
coast	where the edge of the land meets the sea
ferries	ships that carry people and vehicles
festival	celebration where many events take place
Highlands	northern and western areas of Scotland
innard	organ in the body, such as the liver
kilt	woolen skirt worn by men
loch	lake
Lowlands	southern area of Scotland
neeps	rutabaga
oil rigs	metal platforms out at sea where people drill for oil
spinning	making wool into thread or yarn that can be knitted or woven
tatties	potatoes
tourist	person who visits places on trips or on vacation
traditional	something that has been done the same way for many years
uniforms	clothes that people have to wear so they all look the same

Index

More Books to Read

Griffiths, Jonathan. *Scotland*. Milwaukee: Gareth
   Stevens Incorporated, 1999.

Cane, Graeme and Lisa Hull. *Welcome to Scotland*.
   Milwaukee: Gareth Stevens Incorporated, 2002.

The Saltire, or cross of Saint Andrew, is the flag of Scotland.